RISE...

of the Fallen Man—

Deliverance from Bondage and Staying Free

Phil 4:4 Rejoice in the Lord always and again I say rejoice.

H.W. Chip LaPole

Outskirts Press, Inc.
Denver, Colorado

Rise of the Fallen Man
Deliverance From Bondage and Staying Free
All Rights Reserved.
Copyright © 2008 H.W. Chip LaPole
V6.0

Outskirts Press, Inc.
http://www.outskirtspress.com

ISBN: 978-1-4327-3191-5

Library of Congress Control Number: 2008937449

Outskirts Press and the "OP" logo are trademarks belonging to Outskirts Press, Inc.

PRINTED IN THE UNITED STATES OF AMERICA

Why Did I Write This Book and Why Should <u>YOU</u> Read It?

After 26 years of addiction to Cocaine, it is my prayer that God will use the story of the fall and restoration of my life, to change yours ... forever!

- Do you realize that there is a battle going on and it's a battle for your life?
- Do you realize that you have an enemy that walks around SEEKING whom he can devour and YOU are the main course on Satan's menu?
- Do you realize that just because you are saved ... that doesn't protect you from the powers of darkness and in order to protect yourself, you MUST learn to FIGHT, using the

weapons of warfare God has given you?

- Do you realize that even though you have a relationship with God … you could lose fellowship with Him, destroy your life and lose everything?
- Do you realize you may be in bondage and not even know it?
- Do you realize that many Christians are in some form of bondage and that bondage is keeping them from God's best? Bondage is not limited to drugs and alcohol. You can be in bondage to fear, pride, greed, sexual immorality, pornography, licentiousness and the list goes on and on!
- Do you realize you may be a slave to the enemy and not even realize it?

Why did I write this book … I wrote this book to lead you back into the arms of the Lord and to DELIVER you from any form of bondage you may be in.

I also wrote this book in memory of my late wife, who became a casualty of this war for our lives, as she committed suicide September 4, 2004, under the influence of Cocaine, alcohol and other drugs. She chose suicide to set herself free. I chose to write this book so you can "choose life" and LIVE to see your freedom. Several years before her death, the enemy had set his deadly traps for us and little by little (so very subtlety), we began the journey down the path of destruction.

Indeed I was unaware of many things, one of which is the fact that the enemy is patient and willing to wait to entrap us. He is both tactical and strategic in nature. 1 Peter 5:8 gives us a clear picture of Lucifer's vigilance as it warns us to:

"Be sober, be vigilant; because your adversary the devil, as a roaring lion, walks about, seeking whom he may devour" It is critical that you understand this aspect of his nature and the difference between these two approaches, in waging spiritual warfare in the battlefield of your mind.

After reading this book, you will understand his tactics, traps and snares. It will also demonstrate that even a born-again Christian can end up in bondage and out of fellowship with God, if he or she practices a lifestyle of fleshly gratification. Deuteronomy 30:19 says "I have set before you life and death, blessing and cursing: therefore choose life that both thou and thy seed may live." It is my heart's desire that you choose life and that this book leads you out of bondage and into freedom forever.

Chapter 1:

Introduction and the "Inside" Story

I t all began, ever so innocently, which is always how the enemy lures us into bondage. My late wife Toniette and I chose to take a trip to Mexico and stay in an all inclusive resort for a get-away and all inclusive is exactly what this resort ended up being. Both my late wife and myself got saved in Oct 1997 and indeed for a season, our lives where never the same, until we took the bait of satan three years later in 2000, by re-introducing the demon spirit of cocaine into our lives.

I had been a recreational drug user from 1974-1997 (until approximately 6:22 PM, when I received Jesus Christ as Lord and Savior) and marijuana was my gateway drug. Toniette knew very little about drugs and nothing about cocaine. I was the one that first introduced her to cocaine and the one that taught her everything about the effects, preparation, and inhalation … yes I taught her all of it. I introduced her to the drug in 1995 and both of us used recreationally until we accepted Christ as our savior, at which time God took it away from us completely.

I remember that I couldn't understand or even believe what God had truly done in taking my "habit" away from me the first time, when I got saved in 1997. I thought I really had a testimony when that happened as well. Little did I know that I was just beginning the real journey to the destination of near self destruction. Nor when I arrived did I truly believe I would ever be free. As I said before, you can truly be set free and "if the Son sets you free you are free indeed"

From 1997 to the year 2000, neither Toniette nor I had any desire to ever use cocaine (or to drink alcohol which was a generational curse in her family). Indeed God had delivered us both from all forms of chemical dependency.

When we went on our vacation to Mexico, we willfully invited the demon spirit of cocaine back into our lives and began our journey into bondage. Remember – God will always save you from your enemies, but never your friends. Indeed we had once again rekindled our friendship with the demon spirit of cocaine.

Also know that when you are delivered from any form of bondage, deliverance in itself does not make you immune. What I mean by this is that post deliverance freedom then becomes the choice of the individual. Just as in the previous example, we can choose to willfully re-introduce the bondage back into our lives. This also applies to individuals that know Christ and have had a salvation experience and the evidence thereof in their lives. No one is immune to the lusts of the flesh and bondage always comes through the flesh.

So here we are at this beautiful resort on the ocean in Cancun Mexico and the margaritas are flowing like a mighty river. As I sat and reflected upon the beauty of this place, I could hear a voice in the battlefield of my mind saying … so have a drink, what will that hurt. Have just one drink and then call it a night. So, after convincing Toniette that it wouldn't be wrong in the eyes of God if we did, we then repeated the process three times.

If any of you reading this book have made the mistake of drinking Mexican tequila, you will truly appreciate what happened next, as I not only drank several drinks, the bartender talked me into swallowing the Mescal worm in the bottom of the bottle. That experience is exactly what started the downward spiral of our lives. I then proceeded to "score" two hundred dollars worth of cocaine and made the deadly mistake of inviting the demon spirit of addiction back into both of our lives.

I was a blood bought, born again Christian, who stepped out of fellowship with the Lord and I never dreamed it would ultimately cost me everything. "Everything" is defined as losing my wife to suicide, my family relationships, my career, finances, prosperity and self respect. At one point in this journey, I even contemplated suicide, as I had come to the place where I truly believed I had nothing left to live for. Praise the Lord for His commitment to His children, as He spared my life over and over again. He just wouldn't let me go. Now my testimony is very simple "I'M STILL HERE"!

With a net worth approaching a half million, I literally had to lose everything in order to come to the place of brokenness, where I realized the only thing that could set me free and restore my life was God's forgiveness, infinite mercy and unconditional love. Because of the lifestyle of sin I chose to succumb to, I also had to come to the revelation knowledge that "THE CROSS" was enough

I literally went from the penthouse to the jailhouse. I had lost my professional career and job, squandering my life savings and retirement on a $700 a day Cocaine habit, in less than five years. When I ran out of money, I began to sell everything I had to local pawn shops, doing whatever it took to support my habit. I even lived in a homeless shelter at one point, which God provided in my time of need... thank you Jesus. I even owned three cars (I mean owned) at one time. My work car was the oldest vehicle of them all and only two years old, a beautiful loaded SUV.

My credit and personal integrity was so exceptional that I could go into any lender and obtain a signature loan for up to $10,000, no collateral, no title and no security. The Lord blessed me with prosperity year after year, when I was walking with Him; and I even had a year in which I grossed just under $200,000. In addition to tithing, I gave liberally to church, Christian charities, missionaries and any other cause God directed me to give to. Yes, I was a born again Christian and saved by the grace of God, beyond the question of a doubt. God even had even used me to lead thirty-seven people to Christ, before I chose to relinquish fellowship with Him and make cocaine my God. So why am I telling you all this? Because I want you to know that no one, I mean no one, is immune from making the choice to fall away.

I'm being totally honest and warning you, to save you from going through I went through.Jesus said in Revelation 3:15-16 "I know thy works, that thou art neither cold nor hot: I wish thou were cold or hot. So then because thou art lukewarm, and neither cold nor hot, I will spew thee out of my mouth." Hebrews 6:4-6 clearly states "It is impossible for those who have once been enlightened, who have tasted the heavenly gift, who have shared in the Holy Spirit, who have tasted the goodness of the word of God and the powers of the coming age, if they fall away, to be brought back to repentance, because to their loss they are crucifying the Son of God all over again and subjecting him to public disgrace."

Just because you are saved doesn't mean you can't choose to turn your own life into a living hell. I did and I promise you that you don't want to go there. Also understand it doesn't have to be drugs that take you there. You can travel down that same path by embracing any form of bondage and creating an idol in your life, placing a wedge between yourself and your God.

I remember the Lord giving me a mental picture of Him, leaning over the banister of heaven and weeping, as He watched me make choices of my own free will, leading me down the path of self destruction.

The revelation God gave me that enlightened me into making my choice of life over death, was the fact that He is a "big picture" God. He loves us so very much He will literally allow us to destroy our lives (for a season), if He knows in the end that we will come to a place of brokenness and complete surrender, saving us from spending eternity in a burning hell. Indeed God has the big picture in mind and His focal point is where we will spend eternity.

So I am clearly warning you against falling away. Indeed I came close, but by the grace of God, did not come to the place where He hardened my heart and turned me over to the lusts of my flesh. I can clearly remember crying out to the Lord during my bondage to Cocaine, "Lord please don't harden my heart and turn me over to my own lusts." And by the grace of God, He didn't. The most frightening aspect of that time in my life was the fact that He very well could have. I praise Him every day without ceasing for literally saving me from the pit of hell and from myself.

Why did I write this book? I wrote this book as a testimony to the infinite forgiveness and life changing power of almighty God. I wrote this book to warn you, never take the Grace of God for granted and never underestimate the fact that your flesh is utterly sinful and will lead you to death, but only if you choose death. Deuteronomy 30:19 states "I call heaven and earth to record this day against you, that I have set before you **life** and death, blessing and cursing: therefore **choose life**, that both thou and thy seed may live."

Writing this book is my way of making all the fear, loneliness, emptiness, separation, betrayal, tears and brokenness count for something. I'm not writing it for me … I am writing it for you and because YOU are so very special in the eyes of God and that YOUR LIFE IS WORTH LIVING.

Now let me lead you to the freedom Christ died for and into a life of redemption, restoration, hope and fulfillment, as you are freed from whatever holds you back, through the lessons I learned, by the power of the living God, through the shed blood of Jesus Christ. John 8:36

promises "If the Son sets you free, you are free indeed."

Since I surrendered my life to the Lord again, He has been restoring everything, which includes my career, finances and my relationships. You see, Gods word is alive and His promises are true. Once you commit your life to Christ, there is no turning back; and truly the most miserable man in the world is the one that does. Don't learn the hard way like I did; and abide in His love, as "His" love never fails and God "is" love. 1 John 4:8 clearly states "Whoever does not love does not know God, because God is love."

Chapter 2:
Dedication and Acknowledgements

This book is dedicated to my mother Marie (God's little angel), who stood by my side and continued to believe in me, as I went through the "FIRE" and the Lord led me to restoration. I tell everyone that my mother is a walking, breathing example of 1 Corin 13 – "LOVE IS". If it wasn't for her obedience to the Lord in ministering and sustaining me throughout my restoration, I guarantee I wouldn't be alive to write this book, which means you wouldn't be reading it right now. That also means I would never have had the opportunity to minister to you and lead you to freedom, which I most definitely will, but only if you want it for yourself.

My heart goes out to those of you who have ever experienced betrayal and judgment from those whom you have loved unconditionally, despite all of their mistakes in life and have had to endure this behavior practiced as a form of "TOUGH LOVE". Tough Love isn't turning your back on you in your time of need … it is being there for you and walking WITH you through the fire, without enabling you to continue your self-destructive behavior.

Most people embrace the "Tough" part of the definition, but forget the "Love" part, because it means they have to do something unselfish, other than simply walk away from the problem. The "Love" part calls them into "Works" and James 2:20 "Faith without Works is Dead." Hello – did you hear me – Dead! They fail to remember: 1Corn 13:7 "Love bears all things, believes all things, hopes all things and that love never fails"; that God's greatest commandment is to love one another and that God Is Love. I pray that curiosity will lead them to read this book and that they will experience divine revelation (possibly for the first time in their lives) and realize it's ALL about the "LOVE", not the "tough".

Chapter 3:
Am I in Bondage and Can I Be Free?

Yes indeed … you CAN truly be free. John 8:36 "If the Son sets you free, YOU ARE FREE INDEED." This book is about my life and how I have seen this promise become reality after 26 years of addiction to drugs, specifically Cocaine and Crack Cocaine.

In coming to the place of brokenness, where this" Prodigal's son" finally realized that he would either destroy himself by the lusts of his flesh or turn his eye's back to the Savior (yes BACK to the SAVIOR), I had to lose everything. Losing my relationship with God, my wife to suicide, my family, my friends, my prosperity and life savings, my professional career, my peace, my strength and my joy.

Yes indeed … I had to lose everything in order to find the one and only thing that matters for the recovering addict … my FREEDOM from addiction. That freedom came when I finally surrendered my ability to do anything to change my circumstances, realizing I was powerless and submitting by faith to the power of the living God, through the shed blood of Jesus Christ.

Are you taking the grace of God for granted? Is there anything in your life separating you from God's best? Are you playing with "FIRE" in any area of your life? They call it playing with fire because in the end YOU WILL ALWAYS GET BURNT! Do you realize there is a demonic presence in this world whose name is Lucifer, Satan, Beelzebub, the prince of darkness commonly known as the devil, who is trying to destroy … YES DESTROY your life? Do you realize that unless you stop him in his tracks, he can and WILL destroy your life? Do you understand that bondage comes to us in any form we are willing to receive?

Do you believe you are in bondage to anything … do you even know or even worse, do you even care? For a time I didn't care. Yes I knew … but was so immersed in gratifying my "flesh" through drugs that I came to the place that instead of the drug serving me, I became its slave. Yes indeed I was a SLAVE to Cocaine and it became my master, but most importantly … THE SON OF THE LIVING GOD SET ME FREE.

BE ASSURED … THE SON OF THE LIVING GOD WILL SET YOU FREE AS WELL. This book is all about my life, how I came into bondage, the many forms of bondage I served and how the Son of God set me free; and how YOU TOO, CAN BE FREE INDEED.

Chapter 4:
Birthing the Beast

Ow could this happen to me?

- Christian home
- Christian values
- Christian mother (my father just played Christian)
- Christian education (this depends upon how you define Christian)
- Prayed to receive Christ, even as a child – but did you know Him?
  Better yet … did you even care?
- Once saved always saved (rationalizes well if you act like you're saved) … doesn't make a whole lot of sense when you are in bondage, because you don't feel, think or act like you

are saved.

- YOU ... ARE A PRODUCT OF YOUR EARLY LIFE EXPERIENCES ... this rationalizes well if you end up addicted and your childhood was a living hell. DING – doesn't explain things very well if you grew up in a spirit filled, Christian home and ended up addicted. Sounds like more secular hype to me.
- What about bad choices – YOU BET!
  - The best part is that they don't even have to be all yours and that someone else can make them for you ... like your parents, your siblings, Uncle Bob or anyone else that can get close enough to you ... to deliver a life altering Satanic blow.
  - Your "OWN" bad choices – MOST DEFINITELY Deut 30:19 "I call heaven and earth to record this day against you, that I have set before you life and death, blessing and cursing: therefore choose life, that both thou and thy seed may live." Yes indeed ... choose life! It is a whole lot better than going through life as a "dead man walking".

That is - walking through life, out of fellowship with God and disconnected from His vine. John 15:5 "I am the vine; you are the branches. If a man remains in me and I in him, he will bear much fruit; apart from me you can do nothing." So how do we get connected and how can stay that way?

In the beginning ... before salvation, we live without the light, just as I did. I was birthed into religion, sprinkled with the holy water, and girded with the sacraments, Christian grade school and high school. I attended religion class every day for 12 years, during the school year that is. Do you realize that equates to 2,160 hours of Catechism training, which is equivalent in time to a bachelor degree in college? Here's the best part ... I had no CLUE as to who Jesus really was, I thought "born again" was a religious cult and I was discouraged from even owning a bible by "religious" authorities and even the church body itself.

Oh … but indeed, because I received my 1st communion, my confirmation (which I never could find in the bible), made my 1st confession (which IS absolutely true and that was about it; and a one-time "only" commitment), I was taught that I would end up in heaven someday, greeted by St. Peter at the pearly gates. I ask you what is up with that? I was living out of fellowship with God and on my way to a devil's hell. Who will save me from this body of death?

Oh religiosity … how sweet the sound that scathed a wretch like me. I once was lost and nearly drown, deep beneath a deceptive religious sea. Religiosity … man trying to get to God through man made ritual and customs. Praise God for Christianity, our precious Lord and Savior, dying on the cross, making the ultimate sacrifice and coming down from heaven to save a wretch like me (and you my friend). Now that's the real deal!

I can remember sitting at the college bar next to sorority Suzie, looking deep into her innocent and adoring eyes and asking … what religion are you, as if that had any relevance to what I was thinking at the time. I guarantee they were not Godly thoughts. I was a womanizer and I assure you, I had almost as many lines with women as I snorted up my nose during my 26 years of Cocaine abuse. Godlessness exemplified … that is what I was … but just beginning the journey with many more years of evil to perpetuate. What really gets me when I think about it all … is how twisted we can be without even knowing it. How the enemy takes the hurt and emptiness in our own lives and uses it to "reach out and touch", with the kiss of death, the lives of others.

You see, throughout those college years and after, my life was all about gratifying my flesh, in whatever capacity I could, through sexual immorality, alcohol, drugs, pornography, strip clubs … how ever I could. You see, no one ever told me the truth about Jesus, that He was real and not just a bible story character and that accepting Him as Lord and Savior is a choice. No one ever told me that unless I came to the revelation knowledge of Him in my life through a spiritual rebirth, I would end up in a devil's hell for eternity.

Do you understand, there are millions of people today, just like I was, who don't know the truth and are on that same path of destruction? Now be totally honest and ask yourself, do I even care? Better yet, have you ever led anyone to the Lord or even encouraged them to accept Jesus Christ as Lord and Savior? Be honest with yourself and answer another simple question – do I really know Him? I submit to you that anyone who professes to be a Christian MUST have a passion and love for the Lord. I also believe that something is very wrong in a person's walk with God if they don't have a passion for those who are lost. O.K., you may respond that evangelism isn't your spiritual gift.

Matt 28:19 clearly states: "GO YE therefore and make disciples of all nations, baptizing them in the name of the Father, Son and Holy Spirit." I submit to you that if indeed you don't even care, that you need to examine your own heart and confirm that you yourself are saved.

Chapter 5:
Taming the Beast

Note to self – YOU CAN'T TAME A BEAST. Pick up your weapons of spiritual warfare and kill it dead. After you kill it, bury it in the bowels of the earth and never dig it up again.

How do you kill it?

- Don't feed it, starve it – bring it into captivity and literally let it wither away and die. How do I feed it? BY YOUR THOUGHTS, YOUR ACTIONS and YOUR WORDS. By gratifying your flesh when ever it's hungry. Gal 5:16 "Walk in the Spirit and you will not seek to gratify the lust of the flesh." Don't feed your flesh what it wants and starve it to death!

And the last thing anyone usually thinks about ... GENERATIONAL

CURSES! Exodus 20:5b-6 states "For I, the Lord your God, am a jealous God, visiting the iniquity of the fathers upon the children to the third and fourth generations of those who hate me, but showing mercy to thousands, to those who love Me and keep My commandments."

- Generational Curses (passed down from your forefathers, which MUST be broken for you to be free). In my case … this was a big one, numero uno … da big momma. But not just generational curses … actually a "blend" of godless exposure in just the right quantities to yield the end product satan was looking for … my destruction (but I chose to live).

2nd note to self – <u>YOU HAVE GOT TO BE SAVED</u>! Being saved solves all your problems! No, that's not what I said; I SAID YOU HAVE GOT TO BE SAVED – PERIOD! The deception corresponding to this is "getting saved fixes everything and the devil can't touch me." DING – WRONG ANSWER! Getting saved doesn't fix everything, it gets you saved from a devil's hell and gives you the power to overcome evil, period. If indeed you choose to continue to walk in the ways of the world, you become a lifelong CARNAL CHRISTIAN, defeated and useless, never realizing the perfect plan God has for your life.

In fact, until you learn the wiles (tactics) of the enemy and become a mighty spiritual warrior … well, let me put it this way, THERE IS A LEARNING CURVE. Well let's call it a learning slope, mountain, glacier, but remember this: Romans 8:37 "No, in all these things we are more than conquerors through him who loved us." 1John 4:4 "He who is in me (that is in you) is greater than he who is in the world." 2 Corinthians 10: 4-6 "For the weapons of our warfare are not carnal but mighty in God for pulling down strongholds, casting down arguments and every high thing that exalts itself against the knowledge of God, bringing every thought into captivity to the obedience of Christ."

In order to win victory in the "battlefield of your mind" (where the lure and deception to sin begins),

YOU MUST PUT ON THE FULL BODY ARMOR OF GOD:

1.) "Gird your waist with the buckler of truth." Eph 6:14
2.) "Shod your feet with the preparation of the gospel of peace." Eph 6:15
3.) "Place in one hand the shield of faith." Eph 6:16
4.) "Place on your head the helmet of salvation." Eph 6:17
5.) "Place in your other hand and USE the sword of the word." Eph 6:17

Understand that there is a <u>HUGE</u> difference between equipping yourself with these weapons and using them. Using them requires that you act and exercise your faith, fully understanding that these weapons are real, that you do possess them and that when used effectively, they will bring you victory over all of the "wiles" (or schemes, attacks, methods) of the enemy. Understand that he can attack you only through your thought life which penetrates your soul (which is your mind, will and emotions), commonly known as your flesh. So if we "Walk in the spirit we will not seek to gratify the lust of the flesh" <u>Gal 5:16</u>.

So what exactly does that mean and why is "walking in the spirit" so very important for all Christians, especially those who are struggling to be free from bondage to drugs, alcohol or in any other area of their lives. First of all, let's look at some examples of bondage and here are some of them:

- Illegal drugs or alcohol
- Prescription Drugs (yes just because they are legalized does not mean that the individual taking them is free and not living in a state of bondage)
- Relationships and Family
- Anger and rage
- Pornography & Sexual Immorality

- Job and Career
- Mammon (Money)
- Love of Self and Selfishness
- Pride
- Control & Manipulation (The word of God calls it as "witchcraft")
- Verbal abuse

This list is not all-inclusive. During my journey to recovery, I remember asking the Lord to help me understand the deception associated with bondage. I got my question answered loud and clear as God said "Deception comes to us in any form we are willing to receive." That means bondage is available to anyone who is willing to receive and operate in the "deception" associated with it. Let's revisit the eleven examples I gave again … and consider the potential deception associated with each.

Chapter 6:
Bondage & Deception "Satan's Bait"

Illegal Drugs or Alcohol – This is the one that comes easiest for me as it relates to my use of cocaine. I would believe in the lie that I needed to "escape" in order to deal with some stress producing event occurring in my life. I would tell myself that the pain was too great to endure and that by using cocaine, the pain would go away and I wouldn't have to deal with it.

The enemy would tempt me to use. I then would buy into the lie and use. After I would use, I would choose to then receive guilt, condemnation and fear. I was afraid of getting caught and "busted", loosing my job, career, finances, and relationships. My mind became a literal playground for the enemy. Because of these feelings and my inability to cope (although I could have if I would have remained in fellowship with the Lord), I would use again to take myself to a place where it just didn't matter. If I had a disagreement with my late wife, that was another excuse to use. If I had a challenge I had to face at work, yet another excuse to use. Every time I did, I received more demonic oppression, over and over and over again. My life began a downward spiral.

To this day I still fail to understand why it took so long to come to the conclusion, that I would still have the problem and have to deal with it, once I came down from the effects of the drug. There you are ... deception, in that believing the drug was a solution for a "perceived" intolerable problem and the resultant pain from the event occurring in your life.

Revelation came to me finally, after almost destroying my entire life. God gave me two words to live by and those words were – NEVER AGAIN! I must never again use cocaine and indeed I have not. This applies to any form of bondage, as you must stand firm and purpose in your heart ... NEVER AGAIN!

Prescription Drugs – This too is an even easier rationalization ... the deception is believing that you cannot live a "normal and happy" life without the use of a prescribed drug. The worst part about this deception is that the secular world encourages pill popping to solve our emotional problems and that the user believes the drug prescribed is the solution to dealing with the problem.

I am not saying that modern science is not useful for a season, in helping one get to the place of emotional stability in order to promote and accomplish the healing process. What I am saying is that our God is a God of infinite ability and a God of healing. Long term use of mind altering drugs as a coping mechanism is indeed not God's answer.

1 Peter 2:24 says "By His stripes we are healed" and John 8:36 says "If the son sets you free, you are free indeed." The difference between receiving your independence from prescription drugs or not, comes down to one common factor and that is faith. Hebrews 11:6 states "Without faith it is impossible to please God."

Relationships and Family – Yes you can be in bondage to

relationships and even your own family. That my friend is a form of co-dependency. The easiest way to identify if you are in this form of bondage is answer honestly for yourself, is my peace and joy connected to either someone else's or dependant upon interaction with someone else. Rejection and insecurity are powerful tools the enemy uses in both cases, to magnify the desire for both acceptance and approval.

At one time in my life, when I was mercilessly addicted to Cocaine, out of fellowship with God and my family, when I finally decided to receive my freedom, I found myself in bondage to my daughter's approval. I was allowing my peace, joy and strength to be compromised regularly, as I had an insatiable desire to gain back her approval. Problem was I had broken her heart by my falling away from both her and the Lord and I needed to recognize that restoration of relationships is a process, not an event.

One day as I was literally weeping inside from rejection, the Lord spoke ever so clearly to me and said why do I care what anyone else thinks if my actions and words were in agreement with Him? He then told me to trust in Him and He would mend her broken heart, which indeed He has. I'm not saying everything is perfect between myself and my daughter, now (approaching 2 years since I stopped using), but there is a huge difference from where we were at in our relationship with each other and I once again feel the love. Trusting God and healing requires time, which are the two most important principles I need to convey.

Anger and Rage – This condition is initiated based upon unsatisfied expectations, selfishness and inward focus. It begins with offense which is indeed the trap the enemy sets for us. The resultant effect of the unsatisfied expectation, want or desire, is a reaction in anger, instead of operating in "Grace" which we all need.

Another very powerful tool the enemy uses is to create "offense" which leads us into a pattern of forming a "critical spirit". I'm sure you have met people who are nearly impossible to please and on a regular basis point out every little imperfection regarding your personality, choices and actions. This most often stems from low self esteem in the person with the critical spirit, as they find it impossible to give you something they are unwilling to receive for themselves, which is grace and forgiveness.

It is a very true statement that we cannot give something we don't have. Unless we put our past "in the past" and forgive ourselves, we cannot truly forgive others. Lack of forgiveness and grace toward others is what impairs our ability to walk in love. If indeed we don't walk in love, we walk in offense and the resultant effect in many cases is expressed in the form of anger and rage.

Pornography & Sexual Immorality – Indeed this is a huge form of bondage in the US and around the world. It is a fact that that pornography proceeds now exceed the total dollar value of the United States gross national product. Billions of dollars are spent each year via the internet, movies, books and magazines, not to mention related ventures such as prostitution, phone sex etc.

Pornography takes the participant to a place of sexual immorality, where the individual is actually sinning against his or her own body. 1 Corinthians 6:18 states "Every sin that a man does is outside the body; but he that commits fornication sins against his own body."

When pornography enters into a marriage, should that person engage in masturbation, he or she is actually joining or "yoking" themselves with the pornographic imagery. In simple terms they are committing adultery in his or her heart. Jesus said in Hebrews 13:4 "Marriage is honorable in all, and the bed undefiled: but whoremongers and adulterers God will judge."

How can I speak with any authority and credibility regarding this topic and why should you listen to my wisdom regarding being in bondage to pornography … because I was a slave to it for over 30 years of my life. The important aspect of that experience and for you is that I am free and free indeed. John 8:36 "If the Son sets you free, you are free indeed." God's word clearly states in 2 Chronicles 19:7 "Wherefore now let the fear of the LORD be upon you; take heed and do it: for there is no iniquity with the LORD our God, nor respect of persons." Nor respect (or respecter) of persons means God sees us all the same and cares not who you are, in setting you free and giving you your miracle. Therefore, since He set me free, that same freedom is available to you. You too can be free indeed from the bondage of pornography.

Because of a generational curse in my family (yes we are going to talk about generational curses so put your seat belt on if you are unfamiliar with this biblical fact), I became a prisoner to the world of pornography. It all started at a very young age, so young it will even be hard for you to believe. I was seven years old when my father first introduced me to the spirit of pornography. It was a familiar spirit to me as it had been passed down through generations. I am now aware that it was passed down at least three generations, from my grandfather to my father and then on to me, based upon the fact that we all walked in this form of bondage.

Among the many career paths my father pursued during the time he lived my mother and me, I clearly remember his camera shop in Blacks Department Store, Waterloo Iowa. He then moved this store into a "Wal-Mart like" store called Arlans. I remember vividly (but only when I need to and God has purpose for my remembrance, which I will discuss "taking yourself back to the past" later in this book), meeting the spirit of pornography. I don't know if my dad's camera shop was purposed to facilitate what I am about to describe, but there is no doubt in my mind that it surly did.

Do you have your seat belt on … well here goes? I can remember my father carrying multiple photo albums in his car and at work (sometimes even small ones with him), full of pictures he and his friend had taken of women scantily clothed, in the process undressing and in a number of godlessly compromising positions.

I was only seven years old. Now ask yourself honestly, what kind of father in his right mind would show his son that type of graphic material. The answer is much simpler that you think, only a father who was generationally cursed and bound by the demon spirit of pornography. It is important for me to tell you more about my father at this point, to help you understand my relationship with him and conversely, his relationship with me. I also want to give you a little background as to his relationship with my mother and who she was.

My father and mother waited 10 years for my birth. Back in those days (1945-1955), modern science had only identified a limited number of practices that would assist in making a baby. My Mom and Dad used to have to take mom's temperature ... etc, then join together to make a baby. The doctor's gave her vitamins to help ... but that's about it. I will probably never truly appreciate what they both went through during this process, but I know they were totally committed to doing what ever it took. I also believe that the spirit of sexual immorality laid waiting in my father for my birth, as the enemy just loves to break multiple hearts at once and in bringing forth a baby Chip, it did just that.

Once I was born and there were three precious hearts involved, the enemy went to work to destroy the family unit. He also gravitated to the weaker vessel which was in this case my father, because of the generational curse passed down to him. Because he did not have the spirit of God living in him, he was totally defenseless and became a slave to that demon spirit. Understand that that there is a difference between oppression and possession. My father was possessed by the demon spirit of pornography and sexual immorality, not oppressed. Possession cannot take place if the spirit of God lives inside you. Darkness cannot cohabitate in the presence of light as the darkness has to hide.

1 Thessalonians 5:5 "You are all the children of light, and the children of the day: we are not of the night, nor of darkness." 1 Peter 2:9 "But ye are a chosen generation, a royal priesthood, an holy nation, a peculiar people; that ye should show forth the praises of Him who hath called you out of darkness into his marvelous light." Bottom line, in order to get free, you have got to be saved and the Spirit of God must live inside you. Indeed the spirit of God did <u>not</u> live inside my father.

Job & Career – Yes, you can be in bondage to your job and even to your career. This is a very subtle deception and many times the individual in bondage doesn't even realize he <u>is</u> in bondage. Let us look to the word of God again to better understand and validate what I am saying here. Colossians 3:22-25 "Servants, obey in all things your masters according to the flesh; not with eye service, as men pleasers; but in singleness of heart, fearing God; And whatsoever you do, do it heartily, as to the Lord, and not unto men; Knowing that of the Lord you shall receive the reward of the inheritance: for you serve the Lord Christ. But he that does wrong shall receive for the wrong which he has done: and there is no respect of persons."

Indeed this scripture means that we <u>are</u> to work hard at our jobs and obey our leaders. We are to have a pure heart as we walk in obedience and do our jobs with reverential fear of God. After all, it is God who opens the door of opportunity for us, as nothing happens outside of His perfect will for our lives. Our jobs are a gift from God and should be appreciated as such, as if we are working for God himself.

The result from honoring God in our job and career will be abundant prosperity, if indeed we are in "covenant" relationship with Him regarding mammon (that's money). Malachi 3:10-11 "Bring the whole tithe into the storehouse, that there may be food in my house. Test me in this, says the LORD Almighty, and see if I will not throw open the floodgates of heaven and pour out so much blessing that you will not have room enough for it and I will rebuke the devourer for your sakes." Specifically, for those of you who don't know about the tithe, that is giving God 10% of your income (harvest).

I am a witness to this supernatural principle as I personally have been blessed and seen others in this covenant relationship with Him blessed, over and over again. I speak the truth when I say that you just can't out give God. A "giver's" rewards from this relationship come in many forms, promotions, substantial pay increases and a variety of other financial blessings, almost as many as there are stars in the sky (figuratively speaking). This scripture also clearly warns us regarding doing wrong as we will indeed "reap" what we sow.

I have personally experienced this form of discipline and loosing one's job is not something I would ever wish upon anyone. Bottom line, a job is just what it's called; it's a job and we are paid because we are expected to work, which is not only the expectation of our employer, but also the expectation of God.

Now I want to discuss what the job or career shouldn't be. If indeed your job or career is your utmost priority, you have just made an idol out of it and are definitely in bondage to it. Bottom line, God has to be first, then family and then the job. That is God's alignment and He made it that way to enrich and preserve the family unit. Far too many marriages are destroyed by a workaholic husband or wife, who puts the job before his or her marriage. The job shouldn't be more important than your family relationships, especially your spouse and children. Put God first, then your spouse, then your family then the job and career. If indeed you follow God's order, you will be blessed in ALL that you do.

Mammon (Money) 1 Timothy 6:10 says "For the **love** of **money** is the root of all evil". Many Christians confuse the meaning of this and believe it means the accumulation of wealth is the root of all evil and this is simply not true. Money in itself is not the root of all evil nor is the accumulation of wealth. In fact, the accumulation of wealth is biblical. Luke 6:38 says "Give, and it will be given to you. A good measure, pressed down, shaken together and running over, will be poured into your lap. For with the measure you use, it will be measured to you." Also consider Leviticus 26:9 "For I will have respect unto you, and make you fruitful, and multiply you, and establish my covenant with you." Bottom line, God's plan has always been and WILL ALWAYS BE, to provide increase in every aspect of the believer's life. 3 John 2: "Beloved I wish above all things that you may prosper and be in health even as your soul prospers."

Today's society and secular perspective on money directly conflicts with God's laws of prosperity. The key to increase is "giving", not withholding or hoarding. The secular world believes that we need to accumulate all we "can", hide it in a "can" and then "guard the can".

If this is your perspective and you place the value of money before your relationship with God, I guarantee you are in bondage to mammon (money).

Let me give you some examples:

- A willingness to do anything for money (honestly or dishonestly)
- Giving business transactions priority over the Lord
- Coveting other's prosperity
- Stealing
- Being a slave to your job for the sake of money
- Placing money before your relationships (spouse and family)
- Not being a "steward" of what God has given you
- Greed in the accumulation of wealth

Now ask yourself honestly, who do you serve and who is your God?

Consider the words of Jesus in Matthew 6:20 "But lay up for yourselves treasures in heaven, where neither moth nor rust doth corrupt, and where thieves do not break through nor steal" 2 Corinthians 9:7 "Every man according as he purpose in his heart, so let him give; not grudgingly, or of necessity: for God loves a cheerful giver." Indeed the key to prosperity and seizing the blessing of God is not accomplished through greed, it is accomplished through giving. If you struggle to give and find that you are never satisfied with the prosperity God has given you, there is a high probability that you are in bondage to mammon (the love of money). Philippians 4:19 "And my God will meet all your needs according to his glorious riches in Christ Jesus." God is our provision and our sufficiency. Prioritizing the accumulation of wealth above God is idolatry.

1 Corinthians 6:9 says "Know ye not that the unrighteous shall not inherit the kingdom of God? Be not deceived: neither fornicators, norIdolaters."

1 Corinthians 6:10 "Nor thieves, nor covetous, nor drunkards, nor revilers, nor extortionist, shall inherit the kingdom of God."

Love of Self and Selfishness Individuals in bondage to "self", most often do not even realize they are. Indeed it is one of the most subtle traps of the enemy. 2 Tim 3:1-4 says "But know this: There will be terrible times in the last days. People will be lovers of themselves, lovers of money, boastful, proud, abusive, disobedient to their parents, ungrateful, unholy, without love, unforgiving, slanderous, without self-control, brutal, not lovers of the good, treacherous, rash, conceited, lovers of pleasure rather than lovers of God."

So what does "love of self" look like in practice? Very simply, it is a primary focus on one's own needs, with little or no consideration for the needs of others. It is selfishness. Webster defines selfishness as being concerned excessively or exclusively with oneself; seeking or concentrating on one's own advantage, pleasure, or well-being without regard for others.

If an individual is in bondage to "love of self", they have created an idol of self in their lives. This causes severe damage to all relationships they are in, as none of the individuals in relationship with the "lover of self" is ever put first, unless the "lover of self" has something to gain by it. Most importantly if you are in bondage to "love of self", you cannot truly love God, because you are literally in love with yourself. This is not to be confused with loving yourself, which is a totally different subject and the Lord wants us to love ourselves.

So let's discuss the root causes or experiences that result in love of self. Unfulfilled desire for approval as early as childhood, results in insecurity. Because of this, the individual becomes focused upon "self" and gratification of their "unfulfilled" needs. In focusing upon self they create an idol of "self" in their life and desire only that which is important to them and that which gratifies their need for approval.

<u>Deuteronomy 11:13</u> says "And it shall come to pass, if you shall hearken diligently unto my commandments which I command you this day, to **love** the **LORD your** God, and to serve him with **all your heart** and with **all your** soul". If indeed your love of self

exceeds your love for God, you are in a state of idolatry and a huge target for demonic influence. Philippians 2:3-6 clearly warns us "Do nothing out of selfish ambition or vain conceit, but in humility consider others before yourself." Each of you should look not only to your own interests, but also to the interests of others. Your attitude should be the same as that of Christ Jesus: Who, being in the very nature God, did not consider equality with God something to be grasped." When we are in bondage to "love of self" we cannot truly love God.

Pride As with "love of self", pride is also a very subtle trap of the enemy and is most often <u>not</u> recognized by the person in bondage to it. 1 Peter 5:5 clearly states "For God resists the proud, and gives grace to the humble." The fact is God resists the proud. If for no other reason than the fact that God <u>will resist you if you are proud,</u> I would definitely choose humility over pride 100% of the time as God gives "grace" to the humble.

Do you know what the biblical definition of grace is? Grace is the un-merited FAVOR of God. Webster defines favor as regard shown toward another especially by a superior, in the form of approving consideration, special attention, partiality and/or leniency. Let's see, would I want God's favor or would I want Him to resist me, my petitions and desires? That's a "no brainer".

The saddest thing about people in bondage to pride is that they cannot acknowledge their own faults and failures. James 1:24 describes this person very distinctly "and, after looking at himself in the mirror, goes away and immediately forgets what he looks like". Individuals in bondage to pride cannot walk in humility. Therefore they do not have the ability to acknowledge their mistakes and see truth in themselves.

Because of the "pain" associated with failure, which stems from overwhelming criticism and judgment in their early childhood, they have developed an inability to receive truth as a "defense mechanism" to experiencing emotional pain. They are too proud to acknowledge their mistakes and therefore cannot repent.

Forgiveness is contingent upon repentance. Repentance is defined as a conscious "turning away from sin" and turning to God. The individual in bondage to pride has placed the "wedge of pride" between them and their ability to receive the absolute and unconditional forgiveness of God. They must recognize their faults and mistakes in order to come to the place of humility God requires for repentance and forgiveness.

Control and Manipulation The desire for control and manipulation typically originates in an individual who has been abused as a child. Because they had no control of the environment around them growing up, combined with deep seated emotional scars resulting from that environment, they are obsessed with controlling everything around them to defer emotional "pain" at any cost. The primary focus of this need is to control people and the world around them, just as they were controlled and manipulated growing up.

It is "learned" behavior, but also a demon spirit which the word of God associates with witchcraft. Control and manipulation is most often accomplished through several if not all of the following tactics:

- Intimidation
- Fits of anger and rage
- Threats
- Deception
- False witness
- Vain imaginations
- Judgmentalism
- Criticism
- Administering punishment
- Verbal abuse

Control and manipulation also partners with "love of self" as it is the mechanism by which love of self (or selfishness) is gratified. It is true that we are indeed a product of our environment. The good news is that GOD CAN CHANGE THE HEART and this form of bondage can be broken, if the individual is committed to getting free. As with other forms, this type of bondage is so subtle, that the individual doesn't even realize they are a slave to it.

<u>Verbal Abuse</u> – Now I am an expert in this form of bondage, as I was a slave to it most of my life. In fact, if I don't stay vigilant in equipping myself with the full body armor of God every day, I leave myself vulnerable to it. Let me explain how I can claim to be an expert here.

I am a "mouth" in the body of Christ. My "mouth" can bring <u>HUGE LIFE</u> as well as <u>HUGE DEATH</u>; and yours can too. God's word says in <u>Proverbs 18:21</u> "Death and life are in the power of the tongue: and they that love it shall eat the fruit thereof." Speaking death into someone's life, as well as enduring death being spoken into your own life, is one of the worst tasting fruits you can eat. The worst part is when you realize you didn't bridle your tongue and have spoken death into someone else's life.

Jesus said in <u>Luke 17:1</u> "It is impossible but that offences will come: but woe unto him, through whom they come!" Let me tell you, <u>that is one HUGE WOE</u>! That "WOE" opens the door for all sorts of "companion" demon spirits and to tell you the truth, it even gets worse if you are married. Then you are literally speaking death to yourself as Genesis 2:24 states 'Therefore shall a man leave his father and his mother, and shall cleave unto his wife: and they shall become <u>one flesh</u>."

I don't get real sophisticated when it comes to "interpreting" the word of God. Bottom line, I believe it means just what it says and if God said it, that settles it. In this case I believe Genesis 2:24 literally means that when two people enter into a covenant relationship with God in marriage, <u>THE TWO BECOME ONE FLESH</u>! O.K., so what does that mean to you? That means what ever you speak into your spouse's life, you are speaking into your own. <u>You are literally committing spiritual suicide and killing yourself with your own words</u>. Remember where we started, "life and death is in the power of the tongue" and YOU SHALL EAT THE FRUIT OF YOUR WORDS.

Chapter 7:
Know Your Real Enemy

As with everything God does for good, the enemy mimics it and attempts to turn it into evil. Let's go a little deeper here and what I am teaching you will apply to every form of bondage. Understand that God is a God of "rhythms" and "patterns". The word of God gives us a model to follow in establishing Godly rhythms and patterns in our lives.

When Jesus died for our sins, He condemned sin to the flesh. Romans 8:3 says "For what the law could not do, in that it was weak through the flesh, God sending his own Son in the likeness of sinful flesh, and for sin, condemned sin in the flesh". Let me make it clear that this scripture is talking exclusively about the sin aspect being condemned, not the resultant impact we incur from our fleshly decisions. Galatians 6:7-8 "Be not deceived; God is not mocked: for what so ever a man sows, that shall he also reap. For he that sows to his flesh shall of the flesh reap corruption; but he that sows to the

Spirit shall of the Spirit reap life everlasting." Trust me, YOU WILL REAP WHAT YOU SOW IN YOUR FLESH, IN YOUR LIFE, IN YOUR MARRIAGE, IN YOUR RELATIONSHIPS, ON AND ON.

The point I am making here is we do have victory over sin and condemnation though Jesus death on the cross, but we still must face the consequences in this life for our bad decisions. <u>Galatians 5:16-26</u> says "This I say then, Walk in the Spirit, and ye shall not fulfill the lust of the flesh. For the flesh lusts against the Spirit, and the Spirit against the flesh: and these are contrary the one to the other: so that you cannot do the things that ye would. But if you be led of the Spirit, ye are not under the law. Now the works of the flesh are manifest, which are these; Adultery, fornication, uncleanness, lasciviousness, Idolatry, witchcraft, hatred, contentions, emulations, wrath, strife, seditions, heresies, envy, murders, drunkenness, revelers, and such like: of the which I tell you before, as I have also told you in time past, that they which do such things shall not inherit the kingdom of God." I submit this scripture to provide you with a clear understanding of sin and lusts of the flesh.

Once I understood that God has given us a clear list of examples in Galatians 5:16-26, of walking in the "flesh" versus walking in the "spirit", it became much easier to identify exactly where I was at in my walk with God at any given point and time.

2 Corinthians 5:17 says "If a man is in Christ, he is a new creation, old things have passed away and behold all things become new." That means that if you are saved you are a new creation in Christ. You literally have the "mind of Christ". 1 Corinthians 2:16 says "For who hath known the mind of the Lord, that he may instruct him? but we have the mind of Christ." Please understand these truths about your flesh:

- It ALWAYS wants to be gratified (satisfied).
- Gratifying it feels good in your flesh.
- The flesh is ALWAYS at war with your spirit.
- We actually lust to gratify our flesh.

If we choose to walk in the flesh we will reap to the flesh, as a man reaps what he sows. I invite you to review the "lusts of the flesh" in Galatians 5:16-21 again and understand that those who "practice" these things will <u>not</u> inherit the kingdom of God. The other aspect of this truth is that you will have to deal with "reaping" from your actions in this life and I guarantee you absolute misery from that in both this life and the afterlife in a devil's hell.

Galatians 5:22-26 says "But the fruit of the Spirit is love, joy, peace, longsuffering, gentleness, goodness, faith, meekness, temperance: against such there is no law. And they that are Christ's have crucified the flesh with the affections and lusts. If we live in the Spirit, let us also walk in the Spirit. Let us not be desirous of vain glory, provoking one another, envying one another." Once again God offers us a solid example of the "fruit" that comes from walking in the Spirit and once again the law of "reaping and sowing" applies here as well. Now ask yourself, what do you want to reap and what are you sowing?

The enemy wants us to develop sinful habits versus what God wants, which is for us to develop Godly disciplines. Satan is a copycat and his methods will always mimic the basic characteristics of God's, but the fruit is corrupt. So how do we stop the vicious cycle of the flesh? The answer to that is very simple, don't feed it. Which ever you "feed the most" <u>will be the strongest</u> and <u>you will reap exactly what you sow in your life</u>. That is a biblical truth.

Chapter 8:
Breaking the Chains that Bind You

It seems appropriate now, to go to the word of God and provide encouragement, for those of you who **have** the spirit of God living inside you and even those who aren't yet sure. For those of you who have never given your life over to Christ or are uncertain, at the end of this book you will have the opportunity to do just that. If indeed you choose to make that commitment now, I will invite you to go to the "Chapter-10" of this book. I will then lead you through a simple prayer and the best news for you is, all you have to do is mean it with all your heart, but you <u>MUST</u> mean it and indeed the Lord Jesus Christ will come to live inside you, save you from your sins and a devil's hell. You will also begin to walk in the power of God, which means you will have dominion over whatever form of bondage you are in and the ability to <u>get free</u> and <u>stay free</u>.

Now be encouraged in the Lord. 1John 4:4 "Greater is He who is in you than He who is in the World." John 16:33 "I have told you these things, so that in me you may have peace. In this world you will have trouble. But take heart! I have overcome the world." Romans 8:37 "No, in all these things we are more than conquerors through him who loved us." Romans 8:11 "And if the Spirit of him who raised Jesus from the dead is living in you, he who raised Christ from the dead will also give life to your mortal bodies through his Spirit, who lives in you."

Bottom line, if indeed the spirit of God <u>does</u> lives inside you, you <u>can</u> have victory. You have a choice and <u>YOU CAN CHOOSE VICTORY IN JESUS</u>! You must choose freedom and in order to do that you must put your love for the Lord first. Your love for the Lord has to become bigger than your love of self and you must literally crucify that fleshly part of you and remove the idol from your life.

You have dominion over the enemy if indeed the spirit of God lives within you. God will always save us from our enemies, but He will <u>NEVER</u> save us from our friends. Numbers 10:9 "And if you go to war in your land against the enemy that oppresses you, then you shall blow an alarm with the trumpets; and you shall be remembered before the LORD your God, and you shall be saved from your enemies." Now ask yourself honestly, am I in bondage to anything and who are my friends and my enemies?

In order to receive deliverance and freedom from bondage, we must <u>break relationship</u> with that bondage and put God first in that area, take authority and cast it down and away. Luke 10:19 "Behold, I give unto you power to tread on serpents and scorpions, and over all the power of the enemy: and nothing shall by any means hurt you." If Jesus Christ is your Lord and Savior, you have authority. God said it and that settles it! Take authority and cast that godless thing down and out forever! In order to do so, you must end your "relationship' with it.

Anything we put before God is an idol. Now ask yourself honestly, what am I putting before God? It can even be who I am putting before God, which can even be yourself. 1 Corinthians 6:9 "Know ye not that the unrighteous shall not inherit the kingdom of God? Be not deceived: neither fornicators, **nor idolaters**, nor adulterers, nor effeminate, nor abusers of themselves with mankind." Leviticus 26:1 "Ye shall make you no **idol**s nor graven image, **neither** rear you up a standing image, **neither** shall ye set up any image of stone in your land, to bow down unto it: for I am the LORD your God."

Plain and simple, what ever we put before God is idolatry … what ever! It is also clear that if we do so, we will <u>not</u> inherit the kingdom of heaven. I personally believe God has revealed to me, that a person cannot live their life in a state of idolatry, be saved and on their way to heaven. The first requirement is that we MUST be saved and make Jesus Lord of our lives and that means removing all idols.

When we do so, we are born again, not physically but supernaturally and the spirit of God comes to live inside us. I would like to review John 3:1 and following. "There was a man of the Pharisees, named Nicodemus, a ruler of the Jews: The same came to Jesus by night, and said unto him, Rabbi, we know that thou art a teacher come from God: for no man can do these miracles that thou doest, except God be with him. Jesus answered and said unto him, Verily, verily, I say unto thee, except a man be born again; he cannot see the kingdom of God. Nicodemus said unto him, how can a man be born when he is old? Can he enter the second time into his mother's womb, and be born? Jesus answered, Verily, verily, I say unto thee, except a man be born of water and of the Spirit, he cannot enter into the kingdom of God. That which is born of the flesh is flesh; and that which is born of the Spirit is spirit. Marvel not that I said unto thee, you must be born again." Being born again is the first requirement. Unless you are born again, the Spirit of God has <u>not</u> come to live inside you. If this is the case, <u>you are powerless</u> against sin and therefore you will remain in bondage to the enemy.

The second requirement is evidence of a spiritual rebirth. 2 Corinthians 5:17 "Therefore, if anyone is in Christ, he is a new creation; the old has gone, the new has come." Now I want you to ask yourself once more, am I sure that I am born again? If you are uncertain or have changed your mind at this point, we will get you there later, or you can chose to accept Jesus Christ as Lord and Savior right now, by praying the "Prayer of Salvation" in Chapter-10.

In summation, if any form of bondage is operating in your life and if you are struggling with repetitive sinful behavior, this is the revelation that set me free. I finally realized I had created idol(s) in my life. My idols were Cocaine dependency and sexual immorality; and indeed I was choosing to put both of these idols before God. I pray in the name of Jesus right now that the Spirit of the Living God would relentlessly speak this revelation to everyone who reads this book; and that it will find its way to everyone who <u>needs</u> it. I also pray that you choose life over death and do what ever it is you need to, to be "free indeed". John 8:36 "If the Son therefore shall make you free, ye shall be free indeed." For some of you reading this book, that will mean accepting Jesus Christ as your Lord and Savior, for the first time in your life. For others who already know Christ as Savior, that means putting your love for the Lord first and removing everything in your life that comes before Him.

Be encouraged and let not your hearts be troubled. <u>You shall have the victory.</u> John 14:26-27 "But the Counselor, the Holy Spirit, whom the Father will send in my name, will teach you all things and will remind you of everything I have said to you. Peace I leave with you; my peace I give you. I do not give to you as the world gives. Do not let your hearts be troubled and do not be afraid." The Holy Spirit will lead you to your freedom. John 16:33 "These things I have spoken unto you, that in me you might have peace. In the world you shall have tribulation: but be of good cheer; I have overcome the world." **Christ has overcome the world.** Romans 13:14 "But put on the Lord Jesus Christ, and make not provision for the flesh, to fulfill the lusts thereof." Galatians 3:27 "For as many of you as have been baptized into Christ have put on Christ." 1Peter 3:18 "For Christ also hath once suffered for sins, the just for the unjust, that He might bring us to God, being put to death in the flesh, but quickened by the Spirit"

You have no reason to be afraid, nor doubt what God is able to do. Through the shed blood of Jesus Christ, the living sacrifice for sin, you have been set free, if indeed the spirit of God lives inside you.

Chapter 9:
Choosing Freedom

If indeed you have made it through this book and come to this chapter, know this, that you are about to be set free, but you must choose freedom. Also know that <u>John 8:36</u> clearly promises "If the Son therefore shall make you **free**, you shall be **free** indeed." Through the power of the shed blood of Jesus, you can be set free, but you MUST receive Jesus Christ as you Lord and Savior. <u>Romans 8:2</u> also promises "For the law of the Spirit of life in Christ Jesus hath made me free from the law of sin and death."

When you receive Jesus Christ as your Lord and Savior, you are justified in the eyes of God, through Christ's sacrifice on the cross and His righteousness, as Romans 3:23 states "For all have sinned, and come short of the glory of God." Romans 8:1 promises "There is therefore now no condemnation to them which are in Christ Jesus, who walk not after the flesh, but after the Spirit." Bottom line ... you must be saved. Saved from what? Romans 5:12 states "Wherefore, as by one man sin entered into the world, and death by sin; and so death passed upon all men, for that all have sinned." You are saved from condemnation and a devil's hell by receiving the gift of salvation that comes ONLY; through the shed blood of Jesus Christ and His sacrifice on the cross.

When you receive Jesus Christ as Lord and savior you are forgiven for all your sins, past present and future. You are made right in the eyes of God. John 1:12 "But as many as received him, to them gave he power to become the sons of God, even to them that believe on his name." John 3:18 also says "He that believeth on him is not condemned: but he that believeth not is condemned already, because he hath not believed in the name of the only begotten Son of God."

The free gift of salvation through Jesus Christ even gets better, yet as you will live for eternity in heaven. 1John: 13 clearly states "These things have I written unto you that believe on the name of the Son of God; that ye may know that ye have eternal life, and that ye may believe on the name of the Son of God." Wow, eternal life in heaven … now that's an offer you just can't refuse!

Are you ready to "seal the deal"? Are you ready to step out of time and into eternity? If you pray the "Prayer of Salvation" and mean it with all your heart … you will do just that. Your sins will be forgiven; past present and future … and you will have eternal life. YES … eternal means you will live forever in a place called heaven.

You will begin the journey of a lifetime and walk in the power of God. Your words will have POWER and when you speak and stand upon the Word of God, you will have the ability to release POWER from heaven, GOD'S POWER to change your life. You will be set free and have the ability to stay free. Indeed your life will NEVER be the same.

God will hear your prayers and answer them. James 5:16 clearly states that "The effectual fervent **prayer** of a **righteous man** avails much. Note that it doesn't say "avails little" or "nothing". It says the effectual "fervent" prayer of a "righteous" man avails much. When we receive Jesus Christ as our personal Lord and Savior, we are justified and become righteous through the cross and the shed blood of Jesus. Because you are righteous in the eyes of God, He will hear and answer your prayers.

You become a child of the one and only God, creator of the universe. You literally have the power of God available in your life. Romans 8:31 states "If God is with us, who can be against us" Isaiah 43:13 says "Yes, from the time of the first existence of day and from this day forth I am He; and there is no one who can deliver out of My hand. I will work, and who can hinder or reverse it?" NO ONE CAN STOP THE HAND OF GOD – NO ONE! Therefore no one can stop you when you become His child.

You enter into a love "relationship" with God through His Son Jesus Christ. John 14:6 confirms that Christ is the way as Jesus said "I am the way, the truth and the life, no one comes to the father except by me." Receiving Christ as Lord and Savior, IS THE ONLY WAY and yes you can choose to do that right now. It is the MOST IMPORTANT choice you will EVER make. I encourage you to make that choice and receive Jesus Christ as your personal Lord and Savior, RIGHT NOW! 2 Corinthians 6:2 states that "today is the day of salvation"!

Ask yourself honestly, do I know and am I sure of where I will spend eternity when I die. If indeed the answer is NOT heaven, then you will spend eternity in a devils hell. Matthew 10:28 says "And do not be afraid of those who kill the body but cannot kill the soul; but rather be afraid of Him who can destroy both soul and body in hell." The dictionary defines hell as a state or place of woe and anguish, arrived at by the wicked after death. The state or place of total and final separation from God and of eternal misery and suffering, arrived at by those who die without making Jesus Lord of their lives.

The bible clearly states that hell is a real place and many will go there. The King James Bible states in Matthew 7:13 "Enter ye in at the strait gate: for wide is the gate, and broad is the way, that leads to destruction, and many will go in by it."

Let's look at the New Living Translation to provide additional understanding. It explains "[The Narrow Gate] "You can enter God's Kingdom only through the narrow gate." The highway to hell [In Greek, is the road that leads to destruction] is broad, and its gate is wide, for the many, choosing that way.

This scripture has always has always troubled me as I am an "Evangelist" at heart. God created me to lead people to Christ and keep them out of hell. When I realized that "my calling" in life to do so, didn't change the truth in this scripture … I literally wept in my spirit as it literally means that most people ARE going to MISS HEAVEN and end up in hell.

The good news is that you chose to read this book and that you can also choose NOT to spend eternity in hell. Clearly recognize that the choice is COMPLETELY UP TO YOU. Once again I beg you to make the right choice and ask yourself honestly, when I die (a physical death), where will I spend eternity, heaven or hell. The simple truth is unless you make Jesus Christ your Lord and Savior, YOU WILL SPEND ETERNITY IN HELL. PLEASE MAKE THE RIGHT CHOICE AND MAKE IT NOW!

Chapter 10:
The Prayer of Salvation

N ow it is time to make your choice and I am going to lead you in a simple prayer that will change your life and that I can promise. You <u>WILL</u> step out of time and into eternity with God through Jesus Christ when you pray it, but you <u>MUST</u> mean what you pray with all your heart; and YES, <u>it really is that simple</u>.

You must mean what you pray and believe that Jesus Christ died for your sins and that He IS the Son of the Living God. You must also believe that receiving Christ's sacrifice on the cross is the only way to become a child of God. RECEIVING CHRIST IS THE ONLY WAY! Please reflect upon what I have discussed here and then pray this prayer out loud and with all your heart.

FATHER GOD, I KNOW I AM A SINNER. I BELIEVE THAT JESUS CHRIST IS YOUR SON AND THAT YOU SENT HIM TO DIE FOR MY SINS. I BELIEVE THAT THE ONLY WAY TO

SAVE ME FROM A DEVIL'S HELL AND TO BE MADE RIGHT WITH YOU, IS BY ACCEPTING HIM AS LORD AND SAVIOR.

JESUS I NOW RECEIVE YOU AS LORD AND SAVIOR. I RECEIVE YOUR SACRIFICE AND SHED BLOOD ON THE CROSS, FOR THE FORGIVENESS OF MY SINS, PAST, PRESENT AND FUTURE. I BELIEVE IN THE POWER OF THE BLOOD AND RECEIVE THE GIFT OF SALVATION THAT COMES ONLY THROUGH YOU. I BELIEVE THAT YOU ARE THE SON OF THE LIVING GOD AND THAT BY PRAYING THIS PRAYER; YOU WILL SAVE ME FROM A DEVIL'S HELL AND MAKE ME RIGHTEOUS IN THE EYES OF GOD. I BELIEVE THAT YOUR SACRIFICE ON THE CROSS WAS MORE THAN ENOUGH TO SAVE ME AND THAT FROM THIS DAY FORWARD I HAVE BECOME A CHILD OF THE LIVING GOD. THANK YOU JESUS, FOR SAVING ME, THE GIFT OF SALVATION AND FOR ETERNAL LIFE. I RECEIVE THE HOLY SPIRIT AS MY COMFORTER AND BELIEVE THAT YOU NOW LIVE INSIDE ME AND THAT I WALK IN THE INFINITE POWER OF GOD.

I BELIEVE AND RECEIVE AUTHORITY OVER SATAN AND ALL THE POWERS OF DARKNESS. I EXERCISE THAT AUTHORITY NOW AND IN THE NAME OF JESUS, I REMOVE EVERY IDOL AND BREAK EVERY FORM OF BONDAGE IN MY LIFE. I BELIEVE 1JOHN 4:4 THAT "HE WHO IS IN ME IS GREATER THAN HE WHO IS IN THE WORLD," AND STAND UPON THIS SCRIPTURE WHICH IS THE WORD OF GOD. SATAN I CAST YOU DOWN, AWAY AND BEHIND ME. I STAND UPON THE TRUTH AND WORD OF GOD IN JOHN 8:36 "IF THE SON SETS YOU FREE, YOU ARE FREE INDEED." I CLAIM MY FREEDOM FROM ALL BONDAGE IN THE NAME OF JESUS.

FATHER GOD, IN THE NAME OF JESUS I ASK YOU TO BREAK EVERY GENERATIONAL CURSE OF MY FORE FATHERS AND EVERY SOUL TIE IN MY LIFE. I PRAY THAT BY THE INDWELLING OF THE HOLY SPIRIT, I WILL

CLEARLY HEAR YOUR VOICE AND NOW RECEIVE THE POWER, WISDOM, UNDERSTANDING AND DISCERN-MENT TO BE OBEDIENT IN WHAT EVER YOU ASK ME TO DO AND WHERE EVER YOU LEAD ME.

I RENOUNCE EVIL IN MY LIFE, STAND UPON THE WORD OF GOD AND WALK IN YOUR POWER.

LORD JESUS, THANK YOU FOR SAVING MY SOUL. I AM NOW AND WILL FOREVER BE A CHILD OF THE LIVING GOD.

Praise the Lord and congratulations. If you prayed this prayer with all your heart … two things most assuredly happened:

1.) You received salvation through Jesus Christ and were saved from a devil's hell.
2.) You were delivered from what ever form of bondage you were in.

Chapter 11:
Staying Free

Now <u>STAYING FREE</u> and <u>OUT OF BONDAGE</u> is really very simple and can be summarized in two words:

- ## NEVER AGAIN

Whatever it was you were in bondage to have no doubt, <u>YOU HAVE BEEN DELIVERED</u>. STAYING DELIVERED IS NOW YOUR CHOICE.

Several years ago, the Lord gave me a RHEMA word of wisdom, directly from Him. He said "Bondage comes to us in ANY form will are willing to receive.", so guess what … the victory from bondage comes when we DON'T RECEIVE IT! Let me make this crystal clear for you …

- ## DON'T RECEIVE IT!

Unfortunately I can to claim to be an "expert" in this area as well, as God released me several times and I choose to get myself back into bondage. Yes I made that choice and every time I did it, the enemies power to keep me there got stronger. Now the good news is the truth in God's word and that 1John 4:4 "He who lives in you is greater (mightier) than he who is in the world." is a fact. God's power is greater than ALL the powers of darkness combined.

What I don't want you to go through is the physical pain "in this life" associated with being on a roller coaster in getting and staying delivered. That experience cost me a precious life, my prosperity and career (for a very long season) of my life. After walking in blessing and abundance for years, I lost it all and even ended up homeless for a while. Please don't make the same mistake, when you get free … stay free; and the pathway to keeping your freedom are those two simple words … NEVER AGAIN!

Matthew 12:43-45 gives us the clearest example of returning to any form of bondage "When an evil spirit leaves a person, it goes into the desert, seeking rest but finding none. Then it says, 'I will return to the person I came from.' So it returns and finds its former home empty, swept, and in order. Then the spirit finds seven other spirits more evil than itself, and they all enter the person and live there. And so that person is worse off than before. That will be the experience of this evil generation." Please … you have been delivered, now stay delivered, or it will keep getting worse and worse. I still reflect upon how merciful God has been with me. Indeed I have been set free!

How is it that I am staying free? I am staying free by never using cocaine again, nor viewing pornography. Once again – NEVER AGAIN … AND BY THE RENEWING OF MY MIND. Romans 12:2 states "And be not conformed to this world: but be ye transformed by the renewing of your mind, that you may prove what is that good, and acceptable, and perfect, will of God." Indeed this scripture is true … as when we "renew" our minds we no longer find pleasure in sin and have replaced those sinful desires with the things of God. Indeed we are "transformed" just as the word says. I can testify to this truth as indeed it has happened to me. How do you accomplish the renewing of your mind? If you "abide" in Jesus and the word of God (yes you have to read it to abide in it) and you consciously CHOOSE to turn away from sin by keeping His greatest commandments which are clearly stated in Matthew 22:37- 40:

1.) "Thou shall love the Lord thy God with all your heart, with all your soul and with all your mind. This is the first and greatest commandment" (Matthew 22:37-38).
2.) "And the second is like unto it, Thou shall love thy neighbor as thyself. **On these two commandments hang all the law and the prophets."** (Matthew 39-40).

You may be asking yourself, what about the 10 commandments? Here is some divine revelation for you and something I didn't realize, nor did I realize until most recently. You are not and cannot be, nor remain in fellowship with God unless you WALK IN LOVE. Not walking in love defies God's greatest commandment upon which hang all the law and the prophets. **That means when we "walk in love" we keep all the others.**

Chapter 12:
Walking in Love – The Greatest Commandment

E ven if you had the ability to perfectly keep all 10 commandments but didn't walk in love, you would be in a state of conscious sin and out of fellowship with God. 1 Corinthians 13: 1-3 states "If I could speak all the languages of earth and of angels, but didn't love others, I would only be a noisy gong or a clanging cymbal. If I had the gift of prophecy, and if I understood all of God's secret plans and possessed all knowledge, and if I had such faith that I could move mountains, but didn't love others, I would be nothing. If I gave everything I have to the poor and even sacrificed my body, I could boast about it; but if I didn't love others, I would have gained nothing." If we don't choose to walk in love ... WE GAIN NOTHING.

1 Corinthians 13:13 states "Three things will last forever—faith, hope, and love—and the greatest of these is love." MAKE NO MISTAKE ... NOTHING ELSE MATTERS, UNLESS WE ARE

FIRST WALKING IN LOVE.

In order to "abide" or remain in Christ, we <u>MUST</u> walk in love. If you walk in love, you are keeping the greatest commandment and abiding in Christ Jesus. As you abide in the Lord, read and study His word, YOUR MIND IS BEING RENEWED! Therefore, in order to stay free and abide in the POWER of your salvation and Christ Jesus, YOU MUST WALK IN LOVE. If you don't walk in love you won't abide and if you don't abide you won't "bear fruit". If you don't bear fruit, you will be thrown into the fire. Bearing fruit always results from abiding in Christ, but in order to abide (remain in), you must walk in love, as that is God's greatest commandment.

Jesus said in John 15:1-13 (NLV) "[1]I AM the True Vine, and My Father is the Vinedresser. [2]Any branch in Me that does not bear fruit [that stops bearing] He cuts away (trims off, takes away); and He cleanses and repeatedly prunes every branch that continues to bear fruit, to make it bear more and richer and more excellent fruit. [3]You are cleansed and pruned already, because of the word which I have given you [the teachings I have discussed with you]. [4]Dwell(or abide) in Me, and I will dwell in you. [Live in Me, and I will live in you.] Just as no branch can bear fruit of itself without abiding in (being vitally united to) the vine, neither can you bear fruit unless you abide in Me. [5]I am the Vine; you are the branches. Whoever lives in Me and I in him bears much (abundant) fruit. However, apart from Me[cut off from vital union with Me] you can do nothing. [6]If a person does not dwell (abide) in Me, he is thrown out like a [broken-off] branch, and withers; such branches are gathered up and thrown into the fire, and they are burned.

[7]If you live in Me [abide vitally united to Me] and My words remain in you and continue to live in your hearts, ask whatever you will, and it shall be done for you. [8]When you bear (produce) much fruit, My Father is honored and glorified, and you show and prove yourselves to be true followers of Mine. [9]I have loved you, [just] as the Father has loved Me; abide in My love [continue in His love with Me]. [10]If you keep My commandments [if you continue to obey My instructions], you will abide in My love and live on in it, just as I

have obeyed My Father's commandments and live on in His love. [11]I have told you these things, that My joy and delight may be in you, and that your joy and gladness may be of full measure and complete and overflowing. [12]This is My commandment: that you love one another [just] as I have loved you. [13]No one has greater love [no one has shown stronger affection] than to lay down (give up) his own life for his friends. [14]You are My friends if you keep on doing the things which I command you to do. [15]I do not call you servants (slaves) any longer, for the servant does not know what his master is doing (working out). But I have called you My friends, because I have made known to you everything that I have heard from My Father. [I have revealed to you everything that I have learned from Him.] [16]You have not chosen Me, but I have chosen you and I have appointed you [I have planted you], that you might go and bear fruit and keep on bearing, and that your fruit may be lasting [that it may remain, abide], so that whatever you ask the Father in My Name [as presenting all that I AM], He may give it to you. 17This is what I command you: that you love one another."

Not walking in love is sin and a choice because we all have "free will". Free will is defined as the freedom of the will to choose a course of action without external coercion, but in accordance with the ideals or moral outlook of the individual. Indeed walking in love is a choice and we a consciously sinning when we don't.

Chapter 13:

Power Walking with God

W alking in the "Power of God" is a direct result of what you put into it. God desires a personal relationship with you and not a ritualistic, religious one.

In order to have a relationship with someone you must "fellowship" with them. As you draw closer to them, they are drawn closer to you. Mutual trust and a love relationship result from fellowship with God. God is seeking relationship with you and God <u>IS</u> love. 1 John 4:8 states "But anyone who does not love does not know God, for God is love." In order to have relationship with God, we must know Him and to know Him is to love Him. In knowing and loving Him, we most assuredly will walk in His power.

You may be asking, how do I come to know Him and love Him? Following are the disciplines I have formed over the years, to build and keep me in relationship with Him (abiding in Him):

1.) Walk in Love (and <u>NOTHING IS MORE IMPORTANT</u> than this)
2.) Read and Meditate Upon the Word of God (daily)
3.) Confess your Sins (Sin distances us from God)
4.) Keep the Sabbath Holy
5.) Serve the Lord (James 2:20 "Faith without works is dead")
6.) Fellowship with Other Christians
7.) Listen to Christian Music and Stop Listening to Godless Music
8.) Supplement Church Teaching with TV Preaching (but be careful who you watch) Below are some of my personal recommendations:

      a. Joyce Meyer
      b. Creflo Dollar
      c. Charles Stanley
      d. Gregory Dickow
      e. Jentzen Franklin
      f. Marilyn Hickey
      g. T.D. Jakes

Because of your salvation, you now have forgiveness for sin. 1 John 1:9 states:

"If we confess our sins, he is faithful and just to forgive us our sins, and to cleanse us from all unrighteousness." Very simply, un-confessed sin distances us from God. It is amazing how many people neglect to confess their sins and wonder why they remain out of fellowship with God. <u>ALWAYS REMEMBER TO FAITHFULLY CONFESS YOUR SINS DAILY</u>. It is <u>NOT</u> an option, if you seek to "abide" in Him and <u>ABIDING IN HIM IS THE ONLY WAY TO STAY FREE"</u>.

Realize that 1 John 1:9 <u>IS</u> <u>CONDITIONAL</u>. "IF WE CONFESS OUR SINS, HE IS FAITHFUL AND JUST TO FORGIVE US" You must acknowledge your sins to be forgiven. It is an act of humility before God and must not be neglected.

Always remember that God IS love and that love is His greatest commandment. It is my prayer now that God use this book in a mighty way, to change the hearts and lives of millions. That He use the wisdom and principles defined and discussed herein to set every captive free who picks it up and reads it.

- Psalm 30:12 "To the end that my glory may sing praise to thee, and not be silent. O LORD my God, I will give thanks unto thee for ever."

- Philippians 1:6 "Being confident of this very thing, that He who began a good work in you, will perform it until the day of Jesus Christ."

- John 3:16 "For God so loved the world, that he gave his only begotten Son, that whosoever believeth in him should not perish, but have everlasting life."

GLORY BE TO GOD FOREVER!!!

Printed in the United States
132649LV00002B/1-99/P

9 781432 731915